EXTREME CHALLENGE!

PATHFINDER EDITION

By J. J. Kelley and Greta Gilbert

CONTENTS

Paddle to Seattle

They hiked 3,500 kilometers on the Appalachian Trail.
They biked 2,000 kilometers to the Arctic Ocean.
Now two friends face their toughest challenge yet.
Could they kayak from Alaska to Seattle?

© BRIAN A. DIXON

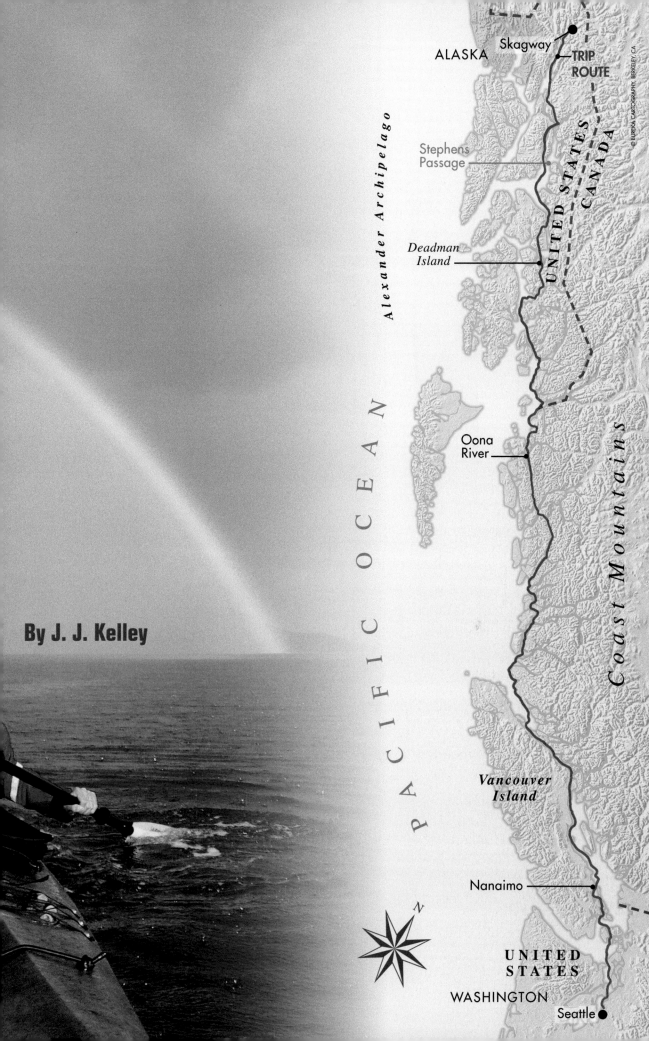

By J. J. Kelley

ALASKA

Skagway

TRIP ROUTE

© EUREKA CARTOGRAPHY, BERKELEY, CA

Stephens Passage

UNITED STATES

CANADA

Deadman Island

Alexander Archipelago

P A C I F I C   O C E A N

Oona River

Coast Mountains

Vancouver Island

Nanaimo

N

UNITED STATES

WASHINGTON

Seattle

Josh Thomas and I stand on a cold, windy beach in Alaska. We're about to start a trip of a lifetime. Our goal is to paddle 2,100 kilometers (1,300 miles) in wooden sea kayaks to Seattle. If all goes well, it should take us three months.

We spent a year planning the trip. Josh built the kayaks, and we practiced paddling. We even flipped our kayaks upside-down in icy water with us inside because we knew rough water could tip us over. We had to know how to roll upright again because it could save our lives.

We gathered gear, too. We needed a tent, sleeping bags, and maps. We packed cameras. We also took a journal to write in every day because we wanted to record everything that happened on our trip.

Getting Ready

Finally, we picked our route (see map, p. 3). We couldn't paddle in the Pacific Ocean because the water is too rough. A storm raging at sea can kick up waves as tall as a house, and that could swamp our boats and smash us against rocks.

We ended up choosing to follow the Inside Passage, which is a watery, wild path that winds between islands along the coast of the Pacific Northwest.

The north end of the Inside Passage starts in Alaska's Alexander **Archipelago**, which is a maze of mountainous islands that lies between the Pacific Ocean and the **mainland**. These islands act like a buffer, or wall. As ocean water flows around them, the land blocks and slows strong waves and **tides**. They block fierce ocean winds, too.

That means the water is calmer in the passage, even when storms are raging. Instead of the house-high waves of the Pacific Ocean, a storm in the Inside Passage might cause only meter-high waves. Seattle, here we come!

© GEORGE WALKER

It took Josh two months to build the kayaks. Here, he glues together the deck of a kayak.

Week 1: Leaving Skagway, Alaska

Bam! A wave hammers the deck of my kayak, and I squint to keep the rain out of my eyes. Winds howl as I paddle forward, but the winds push me back. *Wham!* A second wave hits. I almost flip over. Josh's wrists ache from paddling, and I feel like I can't go much farther. What a first day!

Our second day, we wake to rain and high winds. It's too dangerous to paddle today, so we huddle inside our tent to wait for better weather. We've camped on a hard, rocky beach, so we're wet, cold, and tired.

We soon learn that winds are lightest near dawn, so it's easier to paddle then. Some days, we start at 5 a.m. Yet by the end of the week, we've gone only 113 kilometers (70 miles). Our goal is 168 kilometers (105 miles) a week. At this rate, it'll take us more than four months to get to Seattle! Maybe this trip isn't such a good idea. . . .

A week before our trip, we decide to try out our kayaks. We're at Bear Glacier in Seward, Alaska, and the water is icy cold!

© SPENCER BOYLE

On the fourth night, Josh makes camp in Alaska's rain forest, where Sitka spruce trees can grow up to 95 meters (312 feet) tall.

© J. J. KELLEY

Week 2: Stephens Passage, Alaska

A small group of humpback whales circles our kayaks. When one comes up for air, it blows mist high into the sky. Ugh! The mist smells like rotten fish.

In summer, these whales migrate to Alaska, with some swimming 8,000 kilometers (5,000 miles) just to get here. The whales come partly for the food. There's lots of plankton, small fish, and crustaceans called krill that whales eat. Each whale eats a ton of this food a day. It builds up the whale's blubber, or fat, that the whale will live on through the winter.

One whale darts under me. I feel helpless because it is three times as long as my kayak. It could toss my kayak like a small stick! Air bubbles rise around me and I knock on the kayak. Will the sound keep the whale away? *Phew!* It works.

Week 4: Deadman Island, Alaska

Surprise! It's raining—for the fourth week in a row. I know we've been paddling past one of Earth's few **temperate rain forests**, but I really didn't think a rain forest would be *this* rainy.

Like tropical rain forests, these places are really wet. Moist air blows in from the Pacific Ocean, and nearby mountain ranges trap the moisture along the coast. The water condenses and it rains. Wet fog blankets everything. Some temperate rain forests get 510 centimeters (200 inches) of rain a year!

The air here is cooler than in a tropical rain forest. Different plants and animals live here, too. We see spruce trees and bears, not jungle vines and monkeys.

In a kayak, there's no place to hide from rain, so my fingers wrinkle like raisins. My hands feel raw, and mold grows in my sleeping bag. Then, on day twenty-four, a miracle: No rain! We dry out.

We see many humpback whales on our trip. A breeching one like this could flip our kayaks.

The Inside Passage winds a narrow path past steep mountains in Canada.

Week 6: Oh, Canada!

Wahoo! We just paddled into Canada! Part of the U.S.-Canada border stretches into the ocean. Even bigger news: We're more than a third of the way to Seattle!

By now, we have our routine down: Wake up and eat breakfast. Take down the tent. Pack, paddle, and eat lunch. Paddle, unpack, and put up the tent. Eat dinner and then sleep.

We paddle about eight hours a day. My hands are rough with calluses. I space out as I paddle, stroke after stroke, hour after hour, because it feels endless. My muscles ache. Even the ones I don't use much hurt.

We eat a lot so we have the energy we need to paddle. To add calories, we put butter in everything—rice, fish stew, pasta. I even tried it in my coffee, but is was not so good.

At night, we haul our gear far inland to set up camp. The tide can rise six meters (twenty feet), and we don't want to wake up wet.

The changing tide along the rain forest coast leaves behind bright sea stars and seaweed.

7

Week 7: Oona River, Canada

Bad news. We stop for the night in a small town called Oona River, and a man we meet there tells us: "You're late; the winter storms are coming." He tells us to try again next year.

Is he right? It's late August. Winter may seem far off, and yet we still have a long way to go. This far north, we see signs that the season is changing. The sun sets earlier each day, so we have fewer hours of daylight to paddle, and we're heading into an even rainier season. It also will get colder, windier, and—it seems hard to believe—stormier. After all this, what if we don't make it? I feel sick.

Guess what? Bad weather keeps us in Oona River an extra day. Strong winds uproot trees. The man's words seem to be coming true. After two solid months of being wet and tired, it's hard to stay motivated, and yet we refuse to give up.

Week 10: Vancouver Island, Canada

Our challenging trip continues. One day, the wind is so strong, we paddle less than one mile per hour. Another day, we go farther than ever: fifty-three kilometers (thirty-three miles). The tides help push us along quickly.

We have to paddle a stretch where there are no islands to shield us, so there's nothing between us and the open ocean. A storm right now could be really bad.

Finally, some luck. The seas are calm, and we safely reach Vancouver Island, Canada, which means there are only 483 kilometers (300 miles) more to go. Soon, we'll paddle back into the United States, and maybe we'll succeed after all!

8

Week 13: Seattle!

I see Seattle's skyline and a chill runs down my spine. We did it! It's early October. We faced one last bad storm just after crossing back into the United States. But we beat the winter weather.

Now the adventure is over, and I'm not sure if I'm happy or sad. Josh and I set a goal. We didn't know if we'd succeed. Would it be too far? Would we get hurt? Would we still be friends after such a hard trip? (Yes, we are!)

I've seen and learned so much during this trip. I know what a rain forest really feels like—wet! I found out I really *can* paddle even when my muscles scream "no more." I feel as though I can do anything.

Now there's just one thing left to figure out: Where will our next adventure take us?

Wordwise

archipelago: group of many islands

mainland: main, large landmass of a country, not including islands

temperate rain forest: forest with cool temperatures where it rains at least 152 centimeters (60 inches) a year

tide: regular rise and fall of the ocean's surface about every twelve hours

On a rare sunny day, I'm paddling along the Inside Passage near Nanaimo, Canada. The waves and wind have eroded the land, creating these dramatic sandstone cliffs.

We see our first orcas near Vancouver Island. They travel in pods of up to thirty whales.

Wendy

Booker
and the
Seven Summits

Join a real-life action hero as she climbs some of the world's tallest mountains.

By Greta Gilbert

Picture a hero in an adventure story. She is strong and brave, she is on a **quest**, and she is climbing one of the tallest mountains on Earth.

Wind roars through her five layers of clothing. Her bones ache and her fingers are **numb**. She whistles just to keep her lips from freezing. It is the middle of the day, but the temperature is minus forty degrees. "Not too bad," she thinks, and climbs on.

Meet climber Wendy Booker, the real-life hero of an adventure story. Her quest is to climb the tallest mountain on each continent. Together, these mountains are called the Seven **Summits**.

The Seven Summits

Booker's quest started in Alaska because she wanted to climb Mount McKinley, the tallest mountain in North America. It took two tries before she sweated and trudged all the way to the top. When she finally made it, she wondered, "Now what do I do with myself?"

She made a bold choice: To climb all Seven Summits. Booker soon headed to Africa, where she tackled Kilimanjaro, one of the most famous mountains on Earth.

Each day on Kilimanjaro was different, Booker says. One day, she saw vines that Tarzan might swing on, and another day, she saw trees that Dr. Seuss could have drawn. "I called them poodles on sticks," she says. She loved seeing something new each day.

A year later, Booker climbed Europe's Mount Elbrus. A year after that, she climbed Aconcagua in South America.

Next, she scaled Vinson Massif in Antarctica. Vinson was tough because Booker had to crunch her way through thick snow. She used a special kind of ax to climb on ice.

Then there was the snowstorm when Booker couldn't see anything at all. She and her guide used their hands to find their way back to camp. There, they waited for better weather, and then they tried again.

Yet Vinson has been her favorite climb so far. As she climbed, she realized, "There was nowhere else I wanted to be."

Finally, Booker climbed Australia's Mount Kosciuszko (kah see US koh). It was her sixth summit, so she had just one more to go.

The Invisible Enemy

A hero in an adventure story usually has some sort of enemy, and Booker does, too. It is multiple sclerosis (MS), a serious disease.

MS attacks nerve cells in the brain and spinal cord. These cells send messages throughout the body. Damage from MS means that nerves cannot do their jobs correctly.

MS can make people dizzy, and it can make their muscles hard to control. Or, as in Booker's case, it can make parts of the body totally numb. Yet Booker doesn't let that stop her. Even with her disease, she climbs on.

Help From Friends

Every hero gets discouraged, and when that happens to Booker, she thinks of Jim Cleere's students and former students in Massachusetts. The kids at Donald McKay K-8 School in East Boston have been cheering her on for several years.

Before each climb, the students give Booker a bag of gummy bears. While climbing, she carries a picture of her young fans on her backpack, along with a pink flag that they all signed. At the summit, Booker eats the gummy bears and calls the kids on a satellite phone.

Booker visits the children whenever she can. She talks about her adventures and lets kids check out her **gear**. Each year, she leads a class up a mountain so kids can learn about the adventure of climbing. They practice holding onto rocks and trying to find the right places for their feet.

Climb On!

Soon, Booker will need more gummy bears because she'll face the tallest summit of all—Asia's Mount Everest. If she succeeds, she will be one of few women who have climbed all Seven Summits, and she will be the first woman with MS to do so.

No matter what happens, Booker will climb on. "I want to inspire others," she says. "Especially young people. They should not see **obstacles** as mountains in their way."

You may not climb mountains, and yet you can still be the hero in your own adventure story. Think about *your* Seven Summits and how you can climb them!

Wordwise

gear: the special tools or clothes you need for an activity

numb: without feeling

obstacle: something that makes it difficult to succeed

quest: a journey to get something or do something difficult

summit: the top of a mountain

Wendy Booker climbs a wall of ice on Mount Rainier, Washington.

Design Your Own
EXTREME CHALLENGE!

© MICHAEL NEWMAN/PHOTO EDIT

You don't need to travel the world to face an extreme challenge. You can do it in your own neighborhood! All you need is a challenging goal and a good plan. Try it. You can do it!

Step 1: **Set a challenging goal.** Is there is a nearby hill you want to climb, or a bike or walking path you want to explore? Maybe you would like to reach the top of a special building, or perhaps you would like to cross a certain bridge. Make a goal for yourself that seems a little difficult.

Step 2: **Find an adult partner.** Ask a parent, teacher, or adult friend to join you, and be sure to talk about your goal together to decide the safest way to reach it.

© JASON TODD/RUBBERBALL/CORBIS

© PLUSH STUDIOS/BILL REITZEL/BLEND IMAGES/CORBIS

Step 3: Make a plan. Get a map of your neighborhood, and with your partner, find your route. Then decide how long it will take to reach your goal. Use the chart below to help you.

How far, and how long?

Distance	Time on Foot	Time by Bike
1 kilometer (about 1/2 mile)	15 minutes	4 minutes
1 1/2 kilometers (about 1 mile)	22 minutes	6 minutes
3 kilometers (about 2 miles)	43 minutes	13 minutes

Austin, TX

Mopac
W Martin Luther King Jr Blvd
W 6th St
Lamar Blvd
Guadalupe St
Lavaca Av
State Capitol
S Congress St
E 6th St
Interregional Hwy
E 7th St
E Riverside Dr
S Congress Av
Town Lake
E Cesar Chavez St

0.5   1 Mile
0.5   1 Kilometer

Sources: Robert L. Waters et al., "Energy Cost of Walking in Normal Children and Teenagers," *Developmental Medicine & Child Neurology 25* (1983): 184-188; Diane C. Thompson, "Bike speed measurements in a recreational population: validity of self reported speed," *Injury Prevention 3* (1997): 43-45.

© DON NICHOLS

Step 4: Get Ready. Prepare for your challenge. Will you need any special gear, or do you need to practice a special skill? Be sure to bring food, and plenty of water, too. Remember, the more you prepare, the better chance you have of reaching your goal.

Step 5: Face your challenge. Go for it! There may be parts of the challenge that are difficult, but remember you can ask your partner for help when you need it. When you have completed your goal, celebrate. You did it!

Step 6: Share your experience. Tell friends, family, and teachers about your experience. You may want to write about it in a journal, or online. Don't be shy! Your story can help others reach their own goals!

PHOTOLIBRARY.COM

MEET THE CHALLENGE

Challenge yourself. Answer these questions about how people reach their goals.

1 What goal did Josh Thomas and J. J. Kelley have?

2 Name two challenges the kayakers faced. How did they meet these challenges?

3 What obstacles must Wendy Booker overcome as she climbs a mountain? Why does she do it?

4 What are two questions you have about the Seven Summits? Where can you look to find the answers?

5 How are the people in the articles similar? How are they different?

© ARTVILLE